Letting Myself In

Letting Myself In

Poems by

Anne McCrady

Dos Gatos Press
Austin, Texas

Letting Myself In

Copyright © 2013 by Anne McCrady

ISBN-13: 978-09840399-2-0

Library of Congress Control Number: 2012954974

First Edition

13 14 15 16 17 4 3 2 1

Cover Design: Kristee Humphrey
Cover Photographs: David Meischen and Anne McCrady
Manufacturing: OneTouchPoint – Ginny's

Dos Gatos Press
1310 Crestwood Rd.
Austin, TX 78722
www.dosgatospress.org

Dos Gatos Press is a nonprofit, tax-exempt corporation organized for literary and educational purposes. Our goals are to make poetry more widely available to the reading public and to support writers of poetry—especially in Texas and the Southwest.

With gratitude for
  the company of poets
  my widening circle of family
  the sanctuary of shade

And for Michael
  whose love has invited me
  to our houses of stone and light
  and always to the road ahead

Aubade

Promise

Contents

Letting Myself In

Your cast iron skillet rests behind cabinet doors
with plates and cups, measuring spoons, mixing bowls.
Dishcloths sleep folded in top drawers;
kitchen chairs are gathered close around the table.
The fireplace, hungry for logs and glowing ashes,
crouches cold and vacant against a book-cased wall.
Upstairs, windows watch an open sky
from inside rooms where clothes hang lifeless
and beds crave the weight of slumber.
The carpet, with its uncrushed strands,
is as clean as a Sunday morning suit:
no slips of thread, no paper scraps,
no brittle bits of leaf or grass.
There is no one to scuff muddy feet outside
the door or ring the bell . . . or answer.
But you are here as sure as when I visited
last week, when life still slipped along
as it has for all these years.
I'll gather things that you will want
in your new place and hope you will not hear,
in what I bring, the silence
you have left behind.

In a collage of nascent colors,
the eastern sky bleeds
as it delivers the miracle of a day
for which I have been waiting.

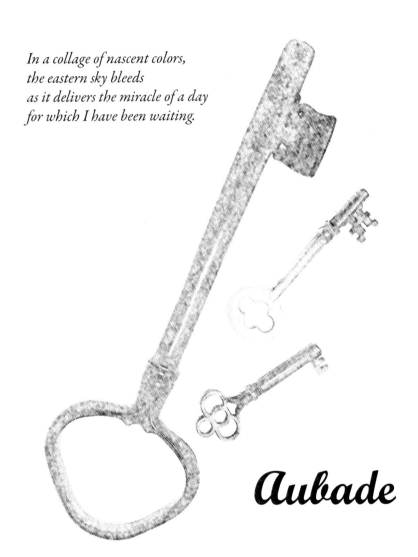

Aubade

Aubade

Of all the times to travel
a new road, why choose now?
How hard it will be
to move from the hearth
just as logs are being hauled inside,
how odd to lift from the hook
beside the door, my jacket—
its weight an informal burden
on my September shoulders.

Turning to go,
I cannot think
what to take along:
a map, a dog, my books.
Maybe it is better
to travel light,
off on my own this time,
each step a reluctant soldier's song
of how hard—oh, how hard—
it is to leave home.

A Stubborn Stillness

One cold oatmeal morning
the road to the next town,
bordered by forests and farms,
drifts into a rural dreamscape:
ponds full and misted,
pastures past sodden,
the sky a gray mat of clouds
framing the day's indecision.

Driving its workday routine,
you notice, in a rain-weighted field,
a fine hickory horse
standing under the only oak,
one caked hoof resting
on its cartilage wedge.
You slow to watch a daddy's girl
in mud-heavy boots
as she nudges open a gate,
raises a metal bucket, beckons
the lone horse to the barn.
Easing his hoof forward
then back again, the animal heaves
a huff of drenched resentment
for the trudge uphill,
shakes the dew from his gray mane,
then slowly starts toward her.

Hungry, too, for what
is next, you turn your gaze,
go, trusting the road
to take you.

Ambitions

They rouse us
from the soft posture
of contented sleep.
Before we know why,
we rise, stumble, shove
our feet into shoes,
hurry toward our hungers:

A new job.
Another degree.
A run for office.
Successful children.
A move to the country . . .
the city . . . the coast.
A puppy. A lover.
An afterlife.

Oh, in our scrambling
for more and more,
what we leave:
our patchwork memories
and deep beliefs, the body
whose embrace holds us
night after night,
spooning our dreams.

Then, one morning, exhausted
by our covetous lives, we see it
is less, not more, that we need.
We can go back to bed . . .
but how will we ever
go back to sleep?

Before You Marry

Drive together out past the places
of mailboxes and mowing.
Cross a wooden bridge
whose metal straps strain, clang,
sing like an old woman finally in love.

Slow around a rutted curve.
Pull up to a clapboard chapel
where patterned windows strain
dyes of ancient hallowed light.
Stop. Say nothing.

Wander the wrought iron churchyard
in the company of velvet-headed oaks
that mourn decades of dead
laid in mounded pairs,
their taken names chiseled in stone.

Whisper the verses. Shiver in the sun.
Listen for the shush of the low wind.
Called by the coming day, look up
and down the empty road.
Feel lost. Feel found. Feel proud.

After an Illness

Inside the shed, she searches
for her bulb shovel, a small spade
with a jagged mouth that opens O's
in the sandy loam to receive tubers
of ruffled daffodils that will bloom
as proof of resurrection next spring.
She moves aside rakes and hoes,
sorts through trowels and nozzles,
sees a raw handle resting on the ground
beside a pair of mud-stiff rawhide
work boots under a season
of wind-silt and pine pollen.

Slipping her house hands
into the crusted boot necks
to move them aside, she gasps
at the limp puppet of a male cardinal
whose scarlet coat is dusted to rust,
neck bent, tail feathers splintered.
Shivering in the damp shade,
she conjures his confusion—flying,
fighting, dying with no escape—
finds herself guilty of the accusations
of a pious mockingbird outside.

She cradles the lifeless visitor,
sets it and the ruined boots aside,
clutches her shovel and bag of bulbs.
Greedy for grace all morning long,
knees deep in dirt, she digs and plants,
prays, makes a way for life to go on.

Dress Rehearsal

The call might come some late morning.
I will be out in the yard weeding
or trimming back the ivy,
some dirty-kneed job of keeping order.
I will have to hurry
to pick up the phone
before it stops ringing,
the person on the other end frantic
to find me, to let me know.
When I sing out hello,
breathless from the race inside,
a flat voice will slam the door
of our lives behind me,
trap me in the dark closet of alone,
offer sympathy as I drop the phone
and run in search of a shirt
that still smells the way you did.

For a New Mother

On good days you will wake first,
the others still inside
their own rounded dreams.
New day on your skin,
you will rest against
an eggshell of solitude
found only at dawn.

Moving in shadows,
you will shiver in the coolness
of a day not yet broken open.
Pulling hair into loops,
rinsing regret from your face,
you will savor the vacuum
of no one's voice calling,
the shy optimism of a day
just beginning to understand
its possibilities.

Everything will be easy,
weightless, peaceful, still.
You will hush even the urge
to call someone to watch with you
the miraculous blood-rush of sunrise.
This will not be for sharing.
Take it. Keep it.
It will be what you need.

Visibility

Like a sail hoisted, a haze
hangs wet and heavy
to obscure my view of the new
beauties: azaleas, bridal wreath,
coreopsis and paintbrush.
The highway beyond our field
is a distant ship channel.
Overhead, a crew of mockingbirds
clings, clangs, an invisible urgent buoy.
Visibility is down to nothing
more than the few feet to the signal flag
on the mailbox. Day waits, keeps watch.
Then, like a gust of sea breeze,
whiteout yields to sun glare.
The morning's mist recedes into heat.
Lanky pine trees appear like ship masts.
The fence along the driveway finds outline.
On the awakening pavement,
the hull of a yellow school bus dawns
over the hill. Birds take flight.
Two dogs cruise the weedy field.
And at the portal of this kitchen window,
lifted from waves of worry,
I am a sailor who can finally see home.

October Rain

In the garden,
leftover moisture clings
to bits of fading growth,
pools on cool, curled vines,
drips in strands of pearls
to the soggy earth beneath.

Time is muffled.
Day cannot climb out
of dawn's damp blanket.
With no breeze, settled,
wood smoke sleeps in.
Live oak flags hang slack,
and pine boughs wait for word.

For now, things can wait.
Like circling geese,
life and clouds float patiently
watching for signs
of a good, hard blow
to dry out the coming day
and open up a clear, cold sky.

Forecast

The temperature has been dropping for days.
Steel slabs of cloud grind the sky into an icy haze.
Snow is predicted; sleet threatens.
Up early—or all night—you are in the kitchen
when I stumble in, tear-swollen and sore
from the mattress only folded out at holidays.
In a practice that is routine but not meant for me,
you make two cups of coffee, sift sugar crystals
and stir, pour in too much cream, scowl.
I smile weakly in uninvited forgiveness.
Weather watchers for three generations—
amateur naturalists, forecasters, note-takers—
we stand on the old back porch to take stock
of the approaching storm, shiver as wet gusts
pack us into a huddle on the porch swing.
Well-meaning friends said, what a shock,
but we both felt trouble brewing months ago,
though no one ever knows for sure how soon.
Breathing the ocher aroma rising like fog
from your cup, you close your eyes, shudder
with each rumble of thunder, stiffen with chill,
wrap yourself like fingers around the familiar
stories we have remembered, told and retold,
sigh the sound we will feel for weeks.
Sipping, then forcing a swallow,
I want to tell you the snow that is coming
will be beautiful, that your grief will fade,
but as I take a breath to speak my consolation,
the wind bears down hard, rattles the screen door
like bones, and all I can think is that, like our coffee,
everything seems to be getting colder.

Ducks at Dawn

Waist deep in dark water
that laps his camo coat
and waders, winter's worst
hinting on the cypress wind,
he needs to bring them in.
For the arrowed flock flying
ninety feet above his blind,
a dozen decoys floating
in the flooded marsh
are not enough
to lure them down to him.
Through barreled wood
and sculpted reed,
cold, fisted fingers fanning
open, he calls, calls, waits, calls.
A nod would give him away.

One by one, green wings turn
and burn their descent
through the morning glare
towards reflected forest gold.
Letting the light frame their flight—
a spiral of broken sky—
he rises through the reeds,
leads, aims, shoots, misses,
but makes his mark
when a drake above him flares.
In the shattered hush,
a flush of feathers spreads
then shreds into a drop
his dog spots with an icy splash
that shatters mudcrust glass
and mirrored sky to shake
the coming day awake—and take
his very breath away.

Early on the Lake

He stares down the metal prow
as it parts curtains
of flannel fog again and again
to reveal an expanse of dark glass
under a suspended droplet sky.
The sputter of his engine bubbles
a path behind him, spits a flat trail
like a fisherman's early morning
walk through dewy shoreline grass.
In the boat, his poles lie as quiet
as the sleepy pup he brings for luck.
He knows like a blind man
the invisible silk road across open water
to his private sweet spots:
a break in the trees, a tuck in the bank,
a bridge post, a deep-water creek bed.
Later there will be whoop and holler,
splash and patter, bass strike,
crappie struggle, but for now he is alone
on the lake with the reverent few
who steer past him like saints,
each seeking a secret
piece of freshwater heaven,
their only blessing
a lifted cap or a silent holy wave.

Camp Song

In the pale light
of a canvas tent dawn,
cicadas kazoo
the last verses of their camp song,
that tinnitus of summer.
Hidden in beds of thin grass,
crickets whistle
their own tinny hymn,
and out by the pond,
amorous tree frogs blurt
wet advances too late now
for evening love.
In the dim air,
dashes of new sun backlight
leftover brown bats catching
the last slow mosquitoes,
and mockingbirds breaking
their full moon fast
fly from feeder
to field to feeder.
A redwing cries;
a woodpecker tattoos
the trunk of a water oak.
Hummingbirds buzz
the butterfly bush.
Jays puncture the air,
and in the oldest pecan tree,
two squirrels run
spiraled wind sprints,
risking the attention
of the new puppy
sleeping at the feet
of a woman who sings
to meet the morning.

Obituary

Our ailing pin oak is down this morning.
No wonder. It has been raining
for six days, after weeks of nothing
but lethal heat and empty skies.
Drought-ravaged and rotting,
the trunk slumps over in a crash of hardwood.
Its spine collapses into soaked soil.

Now it lies in the wet grass,
sprawled in its own lumbering weight,
limbs broken and askew,
roots exposed like stringy entrails:
the season's most recent corpse in the yard,
rain still falling.

Easter Weather

February, and a sudden unearthly spring.
~ Robert Wrigley

Lent came as a torment.
Rainstorms roaring through town,
night after lightning-etched night
in trains of downpours,
making ponds of puddles,
rivers of rivulets,
marshes of manicured yards.
Every morning's sky
was a soaked gray towel
wringing itself out.

Now, after a month of atmospheric
madness, the first day of March
sparkles with sunshine
that jostles beds of jonquils awake
and sends us out to play in the tree house
of new possibilities.

From cobwebbed garden sheds,
rotary tillers tempt us outside
like children calling their mothers
away from aproned chores
to push a swing, sing a rope song,
or dye yard eggs to hide in the spring grass,
its green sudden as grace.

Visited

In the frosted vapors
before dawn, an apparition
in our east field pond: the delicate ghost
of a visiting sandhill crane.

I stand at the window, stunned,
an audience of one
captivated by this single form
on the rose-curtained stage of first light.

Attired in the veil of drifting mist,
she is a model of elegance,
her gray silk silhouette balanced
against the cloudy pinstripe sky.

She is pure ballet: all leg and wing and skirt
danced in lines of winged ink
drawn tangent to the onyx pond
into which she stares, then dips to grip

a minnow with the dagger of her beak.
Swallowing, she bows, accepts my applause,
and, in a breath of feathers, she and the fog
lift into the rising light of day.

Nothing alive is kept inside;
nothing out. We sit together, between
us, a feast: green of every proportion,
the fruit of our private Eden.

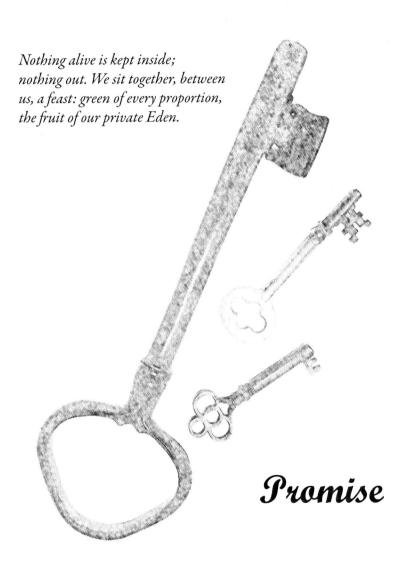

Promise

Promise

On the grayest day
in winter, when even wet boots
would be better than the best
news you have heard lately,
and you need to clear the table
of your latest temptations
to be someplace else,
take out a clean canvas.
Spill the milk of cirrus silk
across a spring-starched sky.
Draw an arrow, a piney line
pointing the way to heaven.
Give it limbs for fletching.
Fill the foreground
with the wild abandon
of azalea blossoms, honeysuckle
trumpets, redbud beads.
Add doe print, coon track,
webs of finest spider weave.
Count the miracles behind you;
consider the ones to come.
Recite the earthy promise
of the buckeye in your pocket:
another April in East Texas
is more than any man's fair share
of grace or good luck.

Spring Inventory

Just before envy tempted me to look away,
I remembered what I had to lose:
Chickweed. Crabgrass. Lamb's ear.
Wild poinsettias. Domesticated ferns.
Five kinds of clover. Ten kinds of vines.
A ditch of dandelions. A field of coreopsis.
Rotting oak logs. Sprouting nandinas.
Sweet gum balls. Sticktights. Bull nettle.
Chinquapin saplings. A longleaf stand.
A volunteer forest. A sprawling hedge.
Apples. Peaches. Pears. Plums.
A vegetable garden. A compost pile.
Rosemary. Lavender. Mint.
A buckeye for good luck.
The biggest pecan in the county.
Crickets. Beetles. Spiders. Slugs.
Fire ants in fortressed mounds.
Snakes, when things get warm.
Frogs. Toads. Minnows. Mosquitoes.
Barn mice. A marauding raccoon.
Bats. Buzzards. Songbirds, all kinds.
Three varieties of woodpecker. Wood.
An alley cat. An occasional stray dog.
Work, unending. Worry, plenty.
Blessings—too numerous to count.

Bent Twigs

Collected, counted, caressed,
they rest in piles awaiting your
command. One by one,
you wet them,
let them bob and soak
until they bend to your bidding.
Gently, your hands mold
them to warp and weave,
wood fibers flexing into curl,
their damp woody skin
becoming supple as a smile.

It is not the kind of work
for those who let shadows pass
without the need for purpose
or those who hurry
through the forest of each day,
but it is perfect for you,
whose given name was a song sung
in the hollow, hungry years
of hickory stick toys
and pine cone dolls.

Now a gray-sky woman
with wickered wisdom,
you keep the old ways
by finding new forms
in field and forest
as you lift dripping twigs
to bend into the curves
of baskets, boxes, handles,
every twisted, limber layer
a lesson woven into the story.

Grackle at Spring Wedding

He sits on the roofline,
a South Texas gargoyle,
his flat boat-tail stiff behind him
like a sail holding him steady
in the undertow
of a heavy Gulf wind.

Spewing his gravelly remarks
in the rude jargon
of a street corner Casanova,
black hair slicked back,
tight pants pulled up high
to tuck in his ridiculous shiny shirt,
he is a nuisance
to well-mannered folks.

Always on the make,
a perpetual bag of hot air,
the epitome of tackiness,
he disrupts the solemn ceremony
taking place below.
A party crasher, a home wrecker,
he is apt to speak up loudly
instead of forever holding his peace.

Even with his constant intrusions,
we allow his presence,
admire his spunk,
offer him as proof
that God has a sense of humor
and knew just the bird
to send to Houston.

Dance Lesson

The roses have given up;
the daisies are spent.
Even our dogwoods are dropping
leaves into the spiked grass,
but against the fence,
the daylilies dance.

In a brash repartee to doldrums
of the summer heat,
their orange and yellow heads
stretch tall to challenge
long-faced rivals
with their wild cavorting.
Every off-stage gust
of wind sends them
bobbing and swaying
in a long-legged chorus line,
their faces radiant.

Other blooms may find a place
in vases on the tables of my home,
but when I need encouragement,
when days are dry and tired,
I look out past the lawn to watch
the daylilies, who know
to turn their faces to the sun
and dance with abandon,
even when no one else hears a song.

Now

Red geraniums
sprawl in prickly pine bark beds,
beaten by the oppressive
assault of summer.
Caught in the crossfire,
shrubs slump in corners.
Vines cling to life.
The grass is forced
into long walks for water.
Mirages in the distance,
clouds are remote
supply lines on the battlefield
of a drought-dry sky.

But among the dead
and dying, something stirs:
wearing black-and-white
flak jackets, two woodpeckers
ladder their way
up the trunk of a dead red oak.
Cunning as war orphans
left to scavenge a life,
they pick and peck,
finding food in the few
caches spared by the sun,
their paired persistence
a lesson in survival.

The Wall

Together, we built it
to mark the perimeter
of our permanence:
a monument to ownership,
that human illusion.
Each morning we watch
the sun slide down
the square-jawed stones,
one perfect tier under another,
each finger-rubbed groove
of gray mortar bleaching
to brilliance as the east trees
allow the slant of rising light.
By noon it becomes
a red clay ridge
dripping with limey
whiteness, humid heat
filling the jagged cracks,
urging each rock
to chip or shift.
Here and there
hang pale green flags
where stashed seeds
have sprouted into weed,
lively reminders
that the world finds ways
to displace us all,
despite our sturdiest
objections to the contrary.

After the Storm

No one is home.
They have all gone looking.
Buildings are beaver dams
of the twister's leftovers.
The roadway is littered
with wind-spirited souvenirs
from a small town turned inside out.
As rescue teams arrive to remove
bodies, they find the macabre:
mannequins wrapped around light poles;
a wig resting on a barber chair
tossed out on the courthouse lawn.
At the gymnasium, metal struts are twisted
into crucifixes; cars have been impaled;
the shopping center is a tortuous sculpture
of clothing, hangers, shattered glass, plastic bags.
As added insult, minutes after the storm,
amidst all the toss and turmoil,
a guilty calm settles over the town's mayhem
with the cool apology of a clear blue sky,
and out along the road, the merciful
go about their work—
policemen and pastors patiently
herding clutches of moaning residents,
who stumble through the rubble
like stunned cattle searching
for a gate back to the familiar.

Natural History

A cicada husk. A tortoise shell.
The cup spun by a hummingbird.
An orb of iron stone, storm-worn
into a mushroom's form.
A giant capped acorn
collected from the apron
of a century oak.
Water oak petrified
into wood-grain stone.
Specimens. Treasures.

When asked her favorite,
she admits it
is a white hen's egg
found on a hollow day,
when she almost stopped
believing in miracles.
Defying the ovulate, it is
round and delicate as a puff ball.
Perfect. Sacred. Impossible.
Proof, she holds now,
lifting her gaze to meet yours,
that anything, anything can happen.

Paradise

By God, the old man could handle a spade.

~ Seamus Heaney

Hoe in brown hands,
he works down one row
of beans and then the next,
grainy mounds of mud
giving way to the slice
and pull of shoulders
strong from fifty-some-odd
seasons of cotton chopping.
A pickup passes, honks.
He uncoils to lift his chin,
take a look, stretch
a smile and wave.
Not sure who it is,
he says it doesn't matter.
Neighbors are neighborly.
He has been on this
corner of East Texas farmland
since his bare feet followed
five older brothers into fields
now sold. Just kept the house
and a little yard to tend.
Across the way, convenience
stores and restaurants stake claim
on the future. Their neon lights
keep him up late at night,
thinking about the black dirt fields
they covered up with concrete.

Before the days are finally hot enough
to plant okra, he says he can taste it
stewed with onions and tomatoes
he started in March. Leaning
on his hoe and thinking toward heaven,
he sighs and posits,
Only God knows 'bout paradise,
but after eighty years on this place,
I figure it'll look right familiar.

103 Degrees

Crepe myrtles petal the burnt soil
with scorched pink ruffles.
Strawberry crowns
shrivel into pinched knots.
Tomato plants tilt
in pungent resignation.
Limp, the leaves
of saplings wilt, then wither,
stripping thin twigs
into crisp circles
of crumbs on the lawn.
Midday in August is a kiln
baking the clay of field and garden
into earthen holds too hard for roots.
Every spot of sun-shot ground
cracks into jagged shards.
Grass bristles, crunches underfoot.
Rain scalds the sidewalk;
steam rises, puddles try to boil.
Even the breeze is a parched blast
fired by the bellowed sun.
Thirst scars the landscape,
bleaches barnwood, wearies women
in box fan houses who look to the sky and sing
Gospel songs about mercy.

Rain. Texas.

The iris of the pond has dilated
all day until, wide-eyed,
it stares back at our relief.
Blind with heat for weeks,
it had become a socket of sand
set under the harsh light
of an unyielding sky.
Now in the blink of lightning
and two nights
of thunderous downpour,
the drought-cracked hollow
has filled to meet
the rattle-grass reaches
of its cattle-mashed banks.
The spillway is a creek,
a river, a muddy cascade
running down the tired face
of the east field, out into rows
tilled and set with seed
before we knew summer
would be so stingy
with its tears
that we would test
the old adage—
In Texas, the only thing
to do about rain
is wait and see.

Rabbit Hole

What goes next, ma'am?
The question is addressed
not to her, the owner
of these cartons containing
eighty years of caring,
but to a middle-aged daughter
recently arrived and looking,
with phone and cash in hand,
as if she must be in charge.

Can I move your car for you?
Her grandson's question suggests
that in the confusion
she has suddenly lost all
benefit of decades of driving
without a single accident
and now needs help
to find her way
down her own driveway.

Surrounded by boxes,
she feels herself
shrinking, shrinking . . .
Watching the movers
hoist her household
belongings out the door
like cargo, she winces
as the house around her
grows larger and larger.

A stranger in this moment
of leaving, like Alice, she longs
to follow the white rabbit
of her resilient heart home.

Under the Canopy

Will they feel the cathedral of these trees,
hear the sonata of mockingbird song,
perceive the liturgy of procreation?
As they pace off boundaries
she marked with privet hedge,
walk dappled pads of grass
that cushion rock and root,
as they describe to one another
the number of trunks
whose girth suggests old age,
whose height is that of heroes,
she hopes they will notice
the history hidden in nests unraveling,
stumps rotting, limbs that have been lost:
the sacred text of life going and gone.
Most of all, when they survey the residence
to get a sense of the place, surmise
right wind, ample rain, good soil,
she hopes they will pray for time
to kneel and know it fully.
In leaving, as they absently pull a leaf
and try to name it, after sizing up
buildings, calculating price,
she longs for them to believe
her own departing assessment:
that the trees in this sanctuary
are a steadfast tribunal of wise elders,
whose girded arms shelter their congregants,
teaching them the dance
that calls sleeping seeds to greenings,
speckled eggs to fledglings,
and heart-bound children
to wonder and delight.

Reimbursement

A hundred times I must have climbed
your legs into this worn-out chenille chair
where roses bloom on dusty papered walls,
my tears dissolving your perfume
when blackberry barbs were buried
deep in swollen fingertips
or angry yellow jackets had defended
roofline nests too well.
Now the chair is mine to pull beside
your bed these afternoons
as we discuss when a merciful God
might take you home to Him.
Biting back my stubborn tears, I rub
the oiled wooden ruts your palms made
as you heaved yourself up from this chair
to start the rolls or find the phone
or head out for the neighbor's house
where death was close and someone called
for you to pray or sit with them,
as I do now for you, my friend,
as I do now for you.

Before the Freeze

When the glaze of icy light
shines from the ground up
to vie for earth's attention
against the feast and flight
of blackbirds on November sky,
sleet falls on the oak-wrapped house
where a graying woman has grown
to believe that, like late life,
this early cold snap is a sign
of shrinking days, a hint of winter,
a forecast of hastening change.

Even so, she says with the sigh
of a seasoned traveler,
if you have a mind to,
there is still plenty of time
to walk a gilded mile
before the first hard freeze.

Dove Season

There is something troubling
about the turned acres
of this farm in September—
fields are fallow; time, tired.
Carrying our inheritance
of grandfather shotguns
across tucked arms,
we each feel it
as we cross fence to fence,
boot-stepping rough clods
spiked with dry cornstalk shreds
as our spindly shadows
stretch across the tiered rows.

Loaded with stories,
a gang of autumn intruders,
we crane our necks
to check the wide horizon,
watch for doves heavy with grain,
seeds of the nodding sunflowers
that face us head-high
like worried peasants
who know the birds
will surely come in
for water on their way
to peach orchard roosts
and be taken easily.

Stopping to rest
in the shade of a low cloud,
I think of the last time
we were here. It was spring,
the corn a waist-deep wonderland
of pale green streamers
that fluttered like May Day ribbons,
the mourning doves no different
than sparrows or killdeers,
just another lilted song
on open-windowed air,
so much summer
still left to live.

Ritual

Each year we stand on this cusp,
this cliff of white rock above Onion Creek,
clinging to the end of summer,
the beginning of fall,
breathing the dry-weed air
on the first day of dove season.
As the sun slumps over the fields,
we hunt for joy, sit for an afternoon,
philosophers in rancher's clothes,
sharing old photographs, new plans,
each held up as proof that life—
like the spring-fed trickle
that snakes through
these chalky ledges—
is constantly changing,
moving, gathering, pooling,
leading us toward whatever waits
downstream.

*At sunset, the glass of our west windows
catches the last splashes of sunlight.
Like a lighthouse lens, the glare
becomes a beacon.*

Dusk

Dusk

. . . both dark and light are true.
~ Kathleen Peirce

Evening deepens to deceive us.
In the thinning orchard, tree trunks darken
sweet green to aging gray to blue-black
as newly set apples ripen into sunset.
Roses, extravagantly rusted buttons,
fade to the memory-laden scent
of your grandmother's dusting powder.
At the edge of the yard, verdigris
wind chimes disappear into chime.
The dog, collar and all, dissolves
into the rope of his nose-up howl
at the empty bowl of the moon.
Inside the house, curtains close
on backyard scenery as dusk drapes
the dimly lit stage. Rooms cool.
Clocks lose track of minute hands
but keep tick-tick-ticking inevitable time.

Even the small child in his quilted bed
becomes a mysterious changeling—
one moment a tearful tyrant,
the next a sleeping cherub.
At this hour, no one knows
the final form of things.

Homesteading

He drove her up a puckered path
cut clean between the cleavage
of the cedared cliffs
and scrub brush climbs
until they disappeared
into the canyon cut
with shadows chasing close behind.

Then he did to her
what he had done
with all this cactus
sand and stone:
he put a fence
around her heart
and called her love
his own.

Sunday in the House He Left

The leftover November light
like supper too long from the oven
has lost its warmth.

She catches the shadow
of her face: a ghost
in the trees beyond the glass.

Confused is a word too deep
in process for her now. Suspended,
she is an odd reflection of old light.

Arms tucked, her bewildered hands
find each other behind her back
as if they have never met.

She'd like to shift her stance
but knows her weight, though slight,
is more than she can bear to move.

Balm of Gilead

In the black wake of tough times,
in the steel grip of never enough,
when my father's life shriveled up
like dried fruit and my mother
had to find her way back,
you were my window to what's next.
At the table of my discontent,
you held up a shiny spoon,
showed me its surface could convex
our futures wide.

Evenings, I can still hear
the lovely exuberance
of our shared bus-ride laughter,
our lipsticked whisperings
as we lay in beds
of pine needles wondering
about boys and clouds and God
and if death really is a victory
for all those who believe.

Mercy

The ground is golden:
a mosaic tableau
of yellow pecan crescents,
umber redbud hearts,
orange sweet gum stars.

A congregant, I cross
the leaf-littered lawn
to the mailbox, ankle deep
in newly downed colors.

The shush
of parchment pieces
gives meter to my steps;
I mark it as I go—
keeping time, keeping time.

Just weeks ago,
we begged the September sky
for mercy, made green promises,
prayed God would ease the heat.

Now a cool breeze has woven
an arboreal altar cloth
in yarns of scarlet, salmon,
coral, saffron and gold,
a temple of seasons,
this blessing.

Winter Woods

After a day in the winter woods
collecting dormant dogwood
saplings, mounds of tree moss,
fallen walnuts, dried grape vines,
I fall exhausted onto the quilt
of a day well spent.
Skin to sheet, I gather into a knot
of woman: arms and legs and breasts
curled in the shifting drape-split
slant of light that crosses my bed,
the spread a sundial.

In the luxurious silence
of the paling of the day,
I watch the fabric of my room
become a purple forest
of lamps and dressers and chairs,
details lost in the dimness.
Drifting, I lose my own light,
fall deep into the shadowed nest
of sleep until I am an acorn
buried deep in linen leafmold,
a seed waiting for the first sign
of sun-sparked things to come.

Snow in South Texas

The palm-lined sand wears white on white.
Powder clings to spiny-limbed coastal pines,
and the evening sea breeze bears
delicate ornaments of crystal
that until now elementary teachers
could only bring to life by dangling
loose-scissored white paper lace
from classroom ceiling tiles
or scotch-taping tissue doilies
to salt-coated window panes.
Now a new vocabulary,
as mothers explain to their children,
in boot-cut Texas metaphors,
the unimaginable marvel
of a White Christmas in Corpus.

When a Town Won't Grow

The frayed edges
of the city limits begin to shrink
so that coming in on the farm-to-market
there are no signs of self-congratulation,
no announcements of coming attractions,
just a rusty invitation to a church
that promises friendly people,
a billboard that advertises
a local used car dealership,
and a population total that is out of date
but at least gives the impression
that a sizeable number of people
still want the blessings of a place
that listens to the whippoorwill
call of dusty pickup trucks hauling families
down to the diner to eat before Mae closes up
and visits her mother at the home
so she can have Sunday free to play
Bingo with her friends at the VFW hall.

Trouble

The mower stirs them up,
she tried to tell him,
the way hard-hearted husbands
she has known stir up trouble
when you least expect it.

He was cutting the east field,
smug with his engine running.
The cloud of them swarmed, stung him
by the dozens, then swung around
to come again, buzzing the summer sun.

Running, calling for her to do something,
he cussed at her for laughing until she cried.
Nursing the swollen knots of strawberry skin,
she offered consolation, but he wanted revenge.
Three beers did the trick for both.

At dusk, he tracked them to a hole
in the hard pack at the back of the hay barn,
snarled with his imagined success.
For a merciful minute, one eye puffed and weepy,
he watched them hover, veer, hover.

Then reckoning—as usual—no regret
was required, he dowsed the spot with oily diesel,
lit the augured dirt and stood over them
smoking a second unfiltered cigarette,
until the last wings withered away.

Weary Warriors

In a corner we lately fenced,
among brambled oaks,
we fight side by side.
Low-hanging limbs
meet the saw blade.
Stumps come up
in clumped crowns.
Greenbrier surrenders
from its climb
high into long leaf pines.
We whack away at root
and rock, stump and stubble.
Little by little,
the last patches
of privet are subdued.

With spoils piled up
and tools laid aside,
we burn a bonfire
of broken branches
and thorny vines:
a pyre to our progress.
Like victorious generals,
we warm our hands against the flames.

As the fire dies to sunset,
we lose our nerve, feel less
like conquerors than crusaders,
who, ravaging the world
they have lately found,
share the doubtful prize
of another piece of Nature civilized.

Water Color

A nesting pair of wood ducks
painted in pin-feathered detail
has inhabited the sunny wall
of our home's entryway,
and I have become an intruder.
The magnificent male,
a yellow and teal block print
version of his dimly speckled spouse,
who quiet, nestles at his side,
preens his extravagant plumage.
Their webby feet are perched
on a fallen hickory log
that breaks the mirror
of their burnished forest pond.
It is always late afternoon, light aslant.
Their orange bills are tucked
into the crooks of their downy necks
as they rest together,
though I imagine that when I am away
they must occasionally
fly out over the wetland hardwoods
or down the creek as a break
from the residential monotony
of my minimalist living room.
Evenings, like a reliable park ranger,
I check to see if they have returned,
half-expecting a family of snapping turtles
to climb from the muddy water onto a nearby snag
or a dragonfly to drift into view.
No. Framed in hickory, tempered glass intact,
there they are: the two of them
settled safely into their feathered repose,
backed by the happy slap of lake bank
and the chit and chatter of woodpeckers
reminding folks like me to keep our distance.

Thoreau in Texas

Watch him realize the freedom
he sought in his New England
wilderness has always been right
outside Kerrville.

See him slip into the stirrup
of a pen between fingertips
as he rides his thoughts
across a low water bridge
of sparkling new ideas,
past the old homestead
of stubborn memories,
along the fence line
of routine and back around
to the corral of life experiences.

Listen to him breathe wide
open spaces into meter,
the rhythm of words laid down
one by one:
stones around a well,
posts along a draw,
peach trees on the ridge,
seeds in a plowed row.

Join him to pause
beside a scrub-brush tank,
to savor the caress of crane shadow,
and to let the music of hummingbird whirr
carry his phrasing into a finished poem
that glints with sunset
in his shining, final line.

County Road 240

Like farmers in red flannel shirts,
sweet gum trees chat in fencerows
beside the winding county road.
Full of stories from the struggles of summer,
they lean against the dusty forest,
their pockets heavy with harvest.
Jostled by gusts of November's insistence,
they practice tossing prickly fruit
into wheat-colored baskets
of waist-high ragweed and Johnson grass.
When a cold blast bears down
like a locomotive, the woods shake out
blankets of live oak leaves
in preparation for company,
and all heads turn to meet the arrival
of the mail order bride:
a blue norther all the way from Canada,
a dry blow sure to stir up a ruckus
as she wraps the last stray lint of autumn
around a line of splintered cedar posts,
clears the evening sky like a broom
and sends stray dogs and husbands
home for supper.

Appetizer

I want the roux to be perfect,
to take all afternoon to brown,
a paste of pale flour toasting
in the oily essence
of carefully kept bacon grease.
I want to watch the heat
soften the tiny cubes
of yellow onion, pale celery,
ivory garlic and bright peppers.
I want to pour in a golden swirl
of broth whose flavors are pulled
from fresh fish pieces and chicken wings,
its dark bouquet a recipe of secret spices.
I want to add a scattering of sweet corn,
a handful of fleshy tomatoes,
a bunch of delicate wagon-wheel okra,
all fresh from my tangled kitchen
garden and warm with afternoon sun.
I want to drop in hot sausage,
red snapper and crabmeat,
to breathe in spicy air
full of Cajun flavor.
Finally, when you lust for it,
I want to be the plump pink shrimp
that is the best part
of your very first bite.

Hunting Party

On a gunbarrel afternoon,
when pine branches are breaking
with ice weight, and walnuts
have frozen into marbled globes,
the men return, camoed and too cold
to joke about Southern frostbite
as they fling a flight of mallards
into the sink to defeather.

Shaking sleet from their shoulders
and pulling mud-caked boots loose,
they unpack vests and pockets
of gum wrappers and red-paper shells,
peel off wet layers of Polartec,
then cotton, as they warm up
to the idea that even torn waders
are worth the taste of duck gumbo.

Huddled around the hearth
of hot biscuits and honey,
limited out, they replay the day
as they unload their stories
to offer one another sweet mercies
for missed shots, dogs
that break early and heated lies
that, deep in the ice of winter,
brothers tell brothers,
as fathers have told sons.

Into Evening

Now the days grow short.
In homage to what's done
as best we could do it,
we set ablaze our mounds
of fallen leaves and twigs.
Against the hastening shadows,
they are bright candles burning
birthday orange and gold.

Leaning on our yard rakes
in a sunset trance, we stare,
hypnotized by the swirl
of dancing, smoky flames
until the faces of children
we once were flicker, flare . . .
and we name again
the things that make us burn.

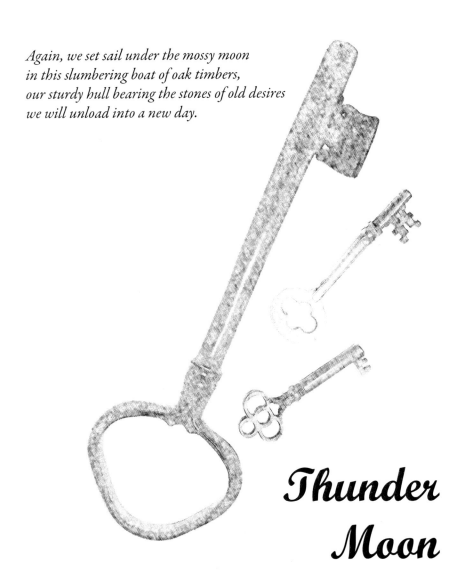

Again, we set sail under the mossy moon
in this slumbering boat of oak timbers,
our sturdy hull bearing the stones of old desires
we will unload into a new day.

Thunder
Moon

Thunder Moon

The Texas summer heat
had become you: all angst and anger.
Cicada song, no more brittle
than your spirit against the blowing grit
of one more minute, one more day.
A rider thrown early. A farmer finished off.
Your fight for a better life lost for good,
the future stifling as a dust storm
on an open-windowed drive west.
You were through, whipped, all done,
until tonight—when, as proof that prayer
can divine God's sweetest mercy,
July gives you its huge Thunder Moon,
a bronze beacon in gold leaf sky,
your heart's darkness lit up
by streaks of silver heat lightning.
Too tired for talk, no taste for tears,
you undress yourself of opinions,
revisions, divisions, complaints.
Stepping out under the banner
of this victorious sky, your spirit
rises to the applause of crickets
and the forgiving coos of mourning doves.
Leaning back to look up into heaven,
you release every sorrow to a breeze
steeped in tea-colored moon shadow,
then drink in deep draughts of hope
sure as this Texas honeysuckled night.

Eclipse

In a move more seductive
than any star
of screen or sky,
you lure me out
to watch you slip
behind a dusty veil
of soft earthshadow.

You pull the pale nightsilk
across your skin
until the sweet curve
of one cool, white shoulder
is all that is left
and then, with a wink,
you are gone.

Dropped Coins

The first day you will wonder,
as you spread plum jelly
on slabs of wheat toast,
if she too is waking
to a day gone cloudy and cold,
if there is anyone to rouse her
and offer the cup of dark coffee
she drank every dawn.

The next day you will think
how odd it is not having her
with you while you watch
movies and cry at the end.
You will lose count
of the weeks; months
will scatter like dropped coins.

Before long, maybe next summer,
as she reads herself to sleep,
you will not be imagining
yourself there, propped up
looking over her shoulder,
your own eyelids heavy with devotion.

In time, whole years will pile up
like laundry or autumn leaves.
As you undress some night,
you will cross your arms
to pull your shirt over your head
and realize you have taken her off too.
Your nakedness will shake you.

Porcelain

After a spring
of good news
gotten too late
to make a difference
the full moon
has waited for me
to rise at midnight
hungry for hope
its lunar face
a porcelain platter
above the pine forest
a luminous bounty set
on a mat of black space
over the hay field table
of our inherited land
a plate so filling
that I take it in
then wince to see it drop
and crack behind the trees
just as splinters of sunlight
thrown from the East
are fused into dayglow
repurposed light that builds
so that I can write
this note to say that
as the solstice turns the world
toward weeks of summer heat
when our passions will flare
then wane into wanting
wanting wanting
that gives way
to the wisdom
of already having

we can know
in darkness and in dawn
everything
yes everything
that is precious
breaks and is remade

Racing to the Moon

Nestled in eggbeds,
warm as brown biscuits stacked and gathered,
they sleep, growing in their dreams,
until the day their covers smother them.

Like sleepy old men, they crawl out,
stretching leathery arms and legs and necks,
stiff and sore, eyes full of birthsleep,
mouths dry as sifted light.

Rousing to the cardiac rhythm
of a tidal mother waiting at water's reach,
they haul themselves from sandy sleepcasts,
pulling back the silica slip.

Trudging across nobs of opened nests,
then out along the moistening sand,
carapace called to sealife,
the wavesong slips beneath them.

Clumsy and cold, with only the moon
to guide them, one after another
they plunge into the surf,
certain of the light that calls their names.

Solstice

In lingering lunarescence
on this, the longest night
of a long year, I watch full
moon magic disappear
over the saw-edge silhouette
of pines that line the west field.
Longing for the light
of what is hidden,
I scribble, erase,
lay lines, move them,
circle truth like the tormented
moth caught in the tether glow
of my desk lamp.
As I struggle, she flutters,
frantic to make sense
of a fallen moon
close enough to touch
but too hot to have.
She beats her paper wings,
throws her tired body
first against the searing light
of the bulb's stark orb
and then against its cold globe.
Beside her, I pummel my pen tip,
scratch words, heave my heart
onto the wide, white moon
of my empty page,
the two of us wrestling, consumed—
one by pitiful instinct,
the other by patent desire.

Listening to Li Po

I am listening to Li Po,
strolling beside the rascal everyone loves
to love, the traveler who knows

the paths to pools of shadow and spikes
of sunset, the one whose lines climb high
into the hills at the slightest sign

of men's work to be done
for the women who feed him and wish
he would come again soon

to drink their rice wine and paint
their wishes with words, his dreamy eyes
dancing with passion,

a poet happy to be drunk
on the nectar of a late lavish rain,
when nothing is more precious

than the face of a familiar woman
and a walk under a new moon.
All this comes in loose haiku

as I smile at the dark-eyed lover
who drinks his beer
and reads Li Po to me.

Sea Call

. . . where the sea meets the shore,
the best of dancing floors.
~ Gregory Orr

With each wave of warm night air,
time rolls to the rhythm of moon pulse:
earth and ocean clasp in a dance
of lean and pull, push and sway
like two salsa dancers caught
in a private trance of taut embrace.
Even the stars lean in, captivated
by the devotion of this coastal pair,
and romanced, we slip away
from our inland dreams,
out to the beach, to part the curtain
of rustling sea oats and clacking dune grasses.
Christened by the spray of night wind,
our bodies murmur and memorize
the pounding of the surf,
the fingertip touch of darkness,
the nuzzle of sweet Gulf air,
the lacy scallops of salt slip
left sparkling on the moonlit sand.

Ordinary Courage

This is not a poem
written on a cocktail napkin
in a place called Chuck's
where women wait
at the bar for chances
they have already taken
and guys who gave up Camels
borrow cigarettes
from middle-aged managers
who sip Chivas
and rub wrinkled foreheads.

That poem is still clinging
to the napkin now folded
and slipped like a tip
into the stained pocket
of a waitress named Terry
who found it on the table
and was pulled back,
heart sliced open,
to 1985, the slapped-hard year
she left home for mercy
but only made it to Houston.

These are not those healing lines.
No, this is another set of stanzas
written later as a celebration
after Terry says that, thanks to my poem
she is moving to make a new start,
and it becomes clear as fog lifting
on an early morning drive east
that no words could match
the honest ardor of a woman
who thinks no one else understands
until I do.

Too New to Each Other

With no proof but passion,
she pushes open the front door
to greet a heat that can only mean
someone has forgotten
to check on the rent house utilities.
His apology tries to turn accusations aside,
but in unfamiliar rooms darkening
into new moon nightfall,
her body, wearing two days
of hard travel, stings
with unanswered fears.

Thunder rumbles.
They hold on to each other
and say what they think
might soothe this trouble come so soon.
Sudden down-drafts
shake the loosely held doors.
Flashes illuminate the empty walls.
As the swollen sky rips open,
a damp breeze breaks the heat.
He laughs; her shoulders soften.
Running outside, she pulls him with her
to wash away the remnants
of what they have come so far to forget.

Rancher, South Texas

The full moon alerts him
with its bright hunger
for the starlit sea,
high tide close enough to smell
the surf—it is almost time.
From the shallow grave
of a widower's fitful sleep,
he listens for the cries
of the old girl calving,
birth still the savage
master it has always been.
The cattle are his inheritance.
This one's bawls call him
to other bad nights,
other hard business.
Before he returns to dreams
of summer pastures
knee-deep in alfalfa,
he says a rancher's prayer
to the God of good fortune.
He does not ask for much:
a good price on hay,
weather that holds,
and that everything,
dear-Lord-everything,
will be all right
in the morning.

Not the Time

We know we have to
get on with it. Grudgingly, we leave
behind the smell of cut grass
and the taste of garden tomatoes
in favor of wood smoke and walnuts.
We put off picnics and fishing trips,
unpack blankets and sweaters,
lie in bed mornings to stay warm.

This is not the time of year
to sell the house or buy a boat,
not the time to hunt up an adventure.
No, this is the season of forgiveness
and homecomings and fires
that burn late into the night,
giving us time to say all the things
we have been too busy to think
but feel the need to say now.

At Fourth & Vine

Tucked into the last booth along the wall
of everyone's and no one's favorite café
on a street where women in dark stockings
and worn brown shoes trudge to laundromats
and drugstores, one or two tired children
in tow, you sit writing out the limits of their lives.

Pens scattered on the table
in front of you, paper already ringed by coffee
cups and pie plate bottoms, you catch and place words
in horizontal lines at first—their placement precise
as the bars on the liquor store windows
across the street—then diagonal additions
in snatches and gasps and dashes,
curving revisions and sudden aspirations.

Watching your efforts for some clue
as to when he should interrupt to warm your cup,
the waiter, a skinny man too young to be right
for you, comes just as your mind wanders out
past the parking lot of lumbering clunkers
on their third engines and truck beds full of work
past the sidewalked rows of fading frame houses
with cluttered yards and potted-plant porches
past the pawn shops and the light poles,
the discount stores and the gas station pumps.

As you try to find the language of possibility,
the café fills with young people who eat and laugh
and old folks who sit to rest with those they love.
Smiling, the waiter, stroking his goatee, asks you:
What else do you need?

Rhetoric

. . . the secret name of death is life again.

~ Mary Oliver

Who among us can argue
the earthy rationale

of grass seeds on a willowy stalk
awaiting the cricket whose clicking
lifted above the night sounds
signals its sadly single state?

Or pin oak acorns pushing
down into sifts of shaded soil,
the damp earth urging
roots to split husks and grow?

Or pools of tadpoles twiddling
temporary tails into rounded nubs
as their paddles grow into legs
and their throats learn to croak?

Or frantic squadrons of blue jays
jammering after their mother
as they hunger to be fed, their eggshells
fallen to nourish ants and worms?

Even when order is undone
by wind and water, fire and frost,
when, confused, we foolishly question
the silence of distant stars
or the orations of dying,
Nature speaks for itself.
Nothing is more persuasive
than the last word.

Days

The best mornings burst open into sunflowers of fried yard eggs, homemade yeast bread and Ball jar mayhaw jelly, swallowed down with coffee sipped in chipped china cups on crepe myrtle mornings when grudges melt like butter in black cast iron skillets. The finest afternoons skitter along behind red dirt children flying bright kites of laughter pulled by chariots of clouds. The most precious seconds are slow ones, when time is a tarnished watch pulled from the overall pocket of a good man who gambles with lies told as gospel as he rewrites his truck farm toils. The nicest evenings are long ones, when justice is shaken out and folded by women who use rumors to air the secrets everyone knows they own. The most blessed hour is the lag time between a lavish meal of reunion leftovers and an after-dinner porch nap, when the prankster joy of a watermelon smile dissolves like sugar into slack conversation and rocked sighs of shared reverie, when a grandboy's eyelids are heavy as his head against an old sofa back as he listens to the exaggerations of three generations of family piled up like pillows—his future and theirs stretching out in front of him like a white rock road that runs out past the orchard to where the wheat patiently waits for the harvest and its farmers to return to the fields.

We Arrive as Strangers

Masons and carpenters by nature,
we make a world of where we are.
Stone by stone, we set in place
the things that keep us grounded:
a window facing east,
trees we planted,
children and their dogs.

Board by rough-edged board,
we build a house to hold our days
and their better companions, our dreams—
a place big enough for abundance
and small enough to insist
we keep only what matters.

As years add to years,
we furnish love-worn rooms
with stories, heirlooms
that we polish
with holiday retellings
and late-night revisions.

And once in a while,
when the earth shifts,
we throw open the front door,
load our stones and boards and stories
and head out into the world
to find the next place that needs
someone to call it home.

About the Author

Anne McCrady's poetry and creative nonfiction appear in journals, anthologies and arts magazines, including *The Texas Review, Texas Poetry Calendar, Borderlands, REAL, Windhover, Concho River Review, Langdon Review of the Arts in Texas,* and *English in Texas.* She won the Edwin M. Eakin Memorial Book Publication Award with *Along Greathouse Road. Under a Blameless Moon* won the Pudding House Chapbook Prize. McCrady's poetry has garnered national recognition, including the NFSPS Founders Award, the Burning Bush Prize, and two Pushcart nominations. Her poetry has been featured by the NPR Twitter feed, the Occupy Poetry website, and the Museum of Fine Art, Houston. Her essay "Speaking the Unspoken" appears in *Wingbeats: Exercises and Practice in Poetry.* McCrady is a judge and councilor for the Poetry Society of Texas, a past editor for *di-verse-city* and former co-editor for *Ginbender.* Passionate about social justice, she is also a frequent speaker and workshop leader, offering literary, inspirational, and storytelling presentations. A life-long naturalist, McCrady received a chemistry degree with a minor in biology from Stephen F. Austin State University. She has spent her life in East Texas and now lives in Tyler, with her husband Mike. More about McCrady's work is available at her website: *InSpiritry: Putting Words to Work for a Better World.*

Acknowledgments

Grateful acknowledgment is given to the following publications, where earlier versions of these poems appeared: **Big Land, Big Sky, Big Hair**—"Grackle at Spring Wedding," "Homesteading," & "Promise." **Blue Hole**—"Days." **Bohemia**—"Thoreau in Texas" (as "Imagine Thoreau in Texas"). **Borderlands**—" Early on the Lake" (as "On the Lake Early." **di-verse-city**—"At Fourth and Vine" (as "Fourth and Vine"), "Dropped Coins," "Listening to Li Po," & "Ordinary Courage" (as "This Is Not a Poem"). **Encore**—"Sunday in the House He Left." **House of Poetry**—"Ambitions," "Before You Marry," & "Natural History" (as "Round"). **My Heart's First Steps**—"For a New Mother." **Poetry Sanctuary**—"Solstice." **Poetry Society of Texas Book of the Year**—"Appetizer," "Dress Rehearsal," "Letting Myself In" (as "After Letting Myself In"), "Racing to the Moon," & "Sea Call." **Rusk County Poetry Society Yearbook**—"Balm of Gilead," "Eclipse," & "Reimbursement." **Sweet Annie & Sweet Pea Review**—"October Rain" (as "October"). **Texas Poetry Calendar**—"Grackle at Spring Wedding," "Homesteading," "Hunting Party," "Promise," "Rain. Texas," "Ritual," & "Thunder Moon." **Under a Blameless Moon**—"Sunday in the House He Left." **Voices Israel**—"Dropped Coins." **Windhover**—"Not the Time" & "Spring Inventory."